Deforestation

Deforestation

Caleb Owens

THE CHILD'S WORLD®, INC.

Library of Congress Cataloging-in-Publication Data
Owens, Caleb.
Deforestation / by Caleb Owens.
p.   cm.
Includes index.
Summary: Briefly describes how the world's forests
are being destroyed, some of the causes and consequences
of this destruction, and some ways of preventing it.
ISBN 1-56766-507-1 (lib. bdg. : alk. paper)
1. Deforestation—Miscellanea—Juvenile literature.
[1. Deforestation. 2. Forest conservation.]   I. Title.
SD418.094   1998
333.75'137—dc21   97-31353
CIP
AC

Photo Credits

© David Hiser/Tony Stone Worldwide: 23
© 1996 DPA/Dembinsky Photo Assoc. Inc: 30
© 1995 Doug Locke/Dembinsky Photo Assoc. Inc: 15
© Dwight R. Kuhn: 16
© Frans Lanting/Tony Stone Images: 29
© 1997 Joe Sroka/Dembinsky Photo Assoc. Inc: 26
© 1993 John Mielcarek/Dembinsky Photo Assoc. Inc: 19
© Mark Kelley/Tony Stone Images: 2
© 1997 Michael D. L. Jordan/Dembinsky Photo Assoc. Inc: 24
© Paul Sisul/Tony Stone Images: 9
© Rex Ziak/Tony Stone Images: cover
© 1997 Rod Planck/Dembinsky Photo Assoc. Inc: 6
© 1992 Sandra Nykerk/Dembinsky Photo Assoc. Inc: 13
© Sue Cunningham/Tony Stone Images: 20
© Zigy Kaluzny/Tony Stone Images: 10

On the cover...

Front cover: Part of this forest has been destroyed for its wood.
Page 2: This logger is using a chainsaw to cut down a forest tree.

Table of Contents

What Is Deforestation?

A forest is a beautiful place. Trees and plants grow thick and green. Sunlight shines through the leaves, and the air is fresh and cool. In the dry forests of the North, you might find squirrels, beaver, and deer. In the rainforests of the South, pythons, parrots, and monkeys are found. But what if something destroyed these forests? All of these wonderful creatures would disappear. This process of destroying forests happens every day all over the world. It is called **deforestation**.

Thousands of years ago, much of Earth was covered with forests. In the North, huge hardwood forests grew for thousands of miles. In the South, thick jungles and rainforests covered the land. Countless animals roamed the world's forests.

Over time, people began living in these wooded areas. To make more room for houses, farms, and cities, they cut down many of the trees. Today, only a few of the first forests remain.

Only one tree still stands in this destroyed forest. ⇒

Why Are Forests Important?

Forests are important for many reasons. One reason is the trees themselves. The forest's trees provide nuts and fruits to eat. But even more important, they give us wood. We use wood for cooking and heating homes. We build our houses and furniture from it. Even the paper in this book comes from wood!

Forests are also important because they protect the ground from **erosion**. Erosion happens when soil is washed away by the rain or blown away by the wind. In the forest, the roots of the trees and plants hold the soil in place.

Erosion has caused a lot of damage in this forest area. ⇒

Forests also clean the air. They produce **oxygen**, which is a gas we need to breathe. Without large forests, Earth would not have enough oxygen for all of its people and animals. Forests give us medicines, too. Many sicknesses can be treated with medicines made from plants. And many of these plants live in the world's forests.

Forests like this one produce air we need to breathe. ⇒

Forests give countless plants and animals an **environment**, or place to live. An environment includes all the things the plants and animals need— soil, water, sunshine, and other plants and animals. If an environment is destroyed, the plants and animals that live there die out. When a type of plant or animal dies out completely, it becomes **extinct**.

Deforestation has caused many animals to become extinct. In fact, scientists think that more than 10 kinds of animals become extinct every day! If deforestation continues, we may never see many types of animals living in the wild.

← This young deer lives in a forest.

Are Forests Strong?

Even though trees and forests look tough, they are easily destroyed. Often trees become weak or sick because of insects or diseases. Other times, fires can sweep through a forest and destroy the plants and trees. But while these things seem bad, they can actually help forests to grow! That is because they clear out old trees and plants so that new ones can grow.

This fire is quickly destroying a Florida forest. ⇒

What Causes Deforestation?

When trees die naturally, new ones grow in their place. But when people cut down trees, they do not always plant new ones. They may turn the land into farm fields or build cities and roads instead. Nature may sometimes weaken forests, but people are the main cause of deforestation.

Why Do People Cut Down Forests?

It seems strange that people would ruin our important forests. But for some people, deforestation seems like the only way to stay alive. In many poor places of the world, people need firewood for heating their homes and cooking their food. They must cut down trees to make their houses, too. And they must cut down trees to make room for their crops. These crops are the only food their families have to eat. So these people believe they must cut down the trees to live.

People cleared this forest area in Guatemala to build homes. ⇒

Where Does Deforestation Happen?

Deforestation happens everywhere. It is a problem for all types of forests—even in very cold areas. Rain forests are being destroyed the fastest, though. In rain forests, people use heavy machines to cut and push trees until they fall over. The machines work much faster than people can. In fact, 12 million rainforest trees can be cut down in one day! In places where machines have cut down the trees, the forests rarely grow back.

⇐ Machines like this loader are used to haul heavy trees away.

Does Deforestation Cause Damage?

Deforestation causes lots of damage. When forests are destroyed, the animals that live there die out. And without trees and plants, wind and rain carry away the soil. There are also fewer trees to provide clean air and wood. But one of the biggest problems deforestation makes worse is the **greenhouse effect**.

In the greenhouse effect, a gas called **carbon dioxide** traps the Sun's heat. This causes Earth to heat up. If Earth warms up too much, weather all over the world could change. Much of the world's carbon dioxide comes from cars and factories. Trees and plants absorb this carbon dioxide and turn it into oxygen. Forests are an important part of this process.

Forest plants and trees are very important to our planet. ⇒

Can We Stop Deforestation?

It is not too late to stop deforestation. Many countries now protect some forests and their animals. While this is a big step, there is still much more to do. We can learn to **recycle**, or reuse, paper and other wood products so fewer trees are cut down. We can also plant more trees when we cut down old ones. If everyone understands and cares about our forests, deforestation can be stopped. Then our beautiful and important forests will be around for many years to come.

← These boys are learning more about a forest near their home. 31

Glossary

carbon dioxide (CAR–bun die–OK–side)
Carbon dioxide is a gas that comes from cars, factories, and other sources. Too much carbon dioxide in the air can cause the greenhouse effect.

deforestation (dee–fore–es–TAY–shun)
Deforestation is the destruction of forests. Deforestation is a serious problem in many parts of the world.

environment (en–VY–run–ment)
An environment is the land, water, plants, and animals that make up a certain type of area. Forests are a kind of environment.

erosion (ee–ROW–zhun)
Erosion happens when soil is washed or blown away. Forests protect the ground from erosion.

extinct (ek-STINKT)
A plant or animal becomes extinct when all of the living ones die out. Deforestation is causing many plants and animals to become extinct.

greenhouse effect (GREEN–hows ee–FEKT)
In the greenhouse effect, carbon dioxide in the air traps sunlight and warms up Earth. Deforestation can worsen the greenhouse effect.

oxygen (OK–sih–jen)
Oxygen is a kind of gas we need to breathe. Forests absorb carbon dioxide and turn it into oxygen.

recycle (ree–SY–kull)
To recycle something is to reuse it. Recycling paper helps to stop deforestation.

Index